The Key to the City

Phoenix Poets
A series edited by Robert von Hallberg

The Key to the City
Anne Winters

The University of Chicago Press
Chicago and London

ANNE WINTERS is the author of a book of translations, *Salamander: Selected Poems of Robert Marteau*. This is her first book of poems.

Library of Congress Cataloging in Publication Data

Winters, Anne.
   The key to the city.

   (Phoenix poets)
   I. Title.   II. Series.
PS3573.I539K4   1986   811'.54   85-8660
ISBN 0-226-90226-9
ISBN 0-226-90227-7 (pbk.)

The University of Chicago Press, Chicago 60637
The University of Chicago Press, Ltd., London
© 1986 by The University of Chicago
All rights reserved. Published 1986
Printed in the United States of America

95 94 93 92 91 90 89 88 87 86   54321

ACKNOWLEDGMENTS

I would like to express my thanks to the Michael Károlyi Memorial Foundation, Vence, Alpes-Maritimes, France, where I wrote a number of these poems; and my gratitude to the memory of its director, Countess Catherine Károlyi.

My thanks also to the Ingram Merrill Foundation, from which I received a grant (1981–82) which helped me complete the most recent section of this book (*The Ruins*).

Poems from this manuscript have appeared in the following magazines and anthologies:

LANDSCAPE AND DISTANCE (University Press of Virginia, 1975)
"Day and Night in Virginia and Boston"

THE NEW REPUBLIC
"Night Wash," "Two Derelicts"

PLOUGHSHARES
"(Detail)," "The Key to the City"

POETRY
"Paolo Uccello," "Alternate Lives," "Pregnant Woman Reading Letter," "Suburban Hours," "Readings in the Navigators," "Demolition Crane," "The Hall of Armor"

SHENANDOAH
"The Armada"

THE THREEPENNY REVIEW
"The Billboard Man"

THE VIRGINIA QUARTERLY REVIEW
"The Illustrated Gazetteer"

Contents

The Ruins

Night Wash

All seas are seas in the moon to these
lonely and full of light.
High above laundries and rooftops
the pinstriped silhouettes speak nightmare
as do the faces full of fire and orange peel.
Every citizen knows what's the trouble: *America's longest
river is—New York; that's what they say, and I say so.*

Wonderful thing, electricity,
all these neons and nylons spun dry by a dime
in the Fifth Street Laundromat. The city
must be flying a thousand kites tonight
with its thousands of different keys.
—Sir, excuse me, *sir?*
Excuse me interfering, but you don't want
to put that in—it's got a rubber backing, see? Oh, not at all . . .

Piles of workshirts, piles of leopard underthings,
it's like fishing upside down all night long, and then the moon rises
like armfuls of thready sleeves. Her voice
rising and falling, her boys folded sideways asleep on the bench:
—Listen, that old West Indian cleaning lady?
Ask anyone here, she never has change.
Come on, she's too wise . . .

Down in the Tombs
the prisoner's knuckles climb like stripes
of paint in the light. He dreams he hears
the voice of a pig he used to slop for his uncles.
It pokes its head
through the bars and says
"Have you brought any beet greens?"

—You can never leave them alone at night. Like today
the stitching overseer says to me
If you can't keep the rhythm missus . . .
I says to him fire
me all you want, I don't take that shit
off anybody. That was a scare though—
you can't always get back on a day shift.

In the moonlight
the city rides serenely enough, its thousand light moorings
the hunted news in their eyes. Even the rivers
are tidal, as sailors and bankers know.
The glass bank of the Chase Manhattan stands dark
over the Harbor. One last
light slowly moving around the top floor.

—No washing machines in the basement, that's
what's the trouble. The laundry would dry overnight
on the roof, in the wind. Well a month ago
you know, some big boys took this twelveyearold
little Spanish girl up there. Then they killed her, they
threw her, six stories down. Listen, the stone age or something
running around on those roofs. So this cop said to me
Your street is the bottom, he actually
said that to me. So what could I say—that it's great?

On the folding table the same
gestures repeat, smoothing and folding
the same ancient shirt. Or the old West Indian cleaning lady
pretending to finger her pockets for change. At midnight she'll prop
her grey spaghetti mop and glide toward you
in her black cotton trousers, her black
lavender face tilted up. Very clearly
she says to the world in dream-language
I mean to live.

Two Derelicts

Two derelicts, scouring for butts on hands and knees,
stirred up a question I'd left hanging years ago
when I was a student. Fifth Avenue: I was on a bench
when I saw them, the park side, under the trees,
and they were pincering cigarette butts from between
the grey glacial cobbles. Rag man, rag woman,
I could hear their sweatstiff coats rustle on the unfinished
undersides of the benchboards; saw a rotting bandana,
a brownscaled neck, strange tails of hair. They were foraging
swiftly, jerkily, with a horrible alertness
for the ground with its detail of litter. Eyes raised
rarely—but everyone's intercepted it
sometime, that wooden look of hate
that breaks their bodies out in open sores,
raying the eyes, the lips seamed dark as fists—
I sat still, in my forest clearing, though surely
invisible to them: woman with paper, purse,
a city immeasurably far behind them,
so many lightyears out from their last port.
Barely a point of reference. They crawled so near,
not looking up, their odor filled my air.

That started me off, and the earlier thing, the question,
was when I was living poor (but fat,
from solitary gorgings on second-day baked goods)
just off the Bowery. I crossed it every morning
to class or jobs: barelegged, fatlegged, blue
in the winter, always depressed and euphoric
with student poverty (the traveler's
unconscious *I'll only be here once*). The moment I mean,
my legs had just callipered a stale bundle
with a face my eyes jerked away from, red porous mound
in brown twiggery, two green ropes of snot.
I could smell him, though, and the derelicts brought
that smell back where I sat

where my poor-years had placed me, free on my lunch hour—at ease.
But what set its seal on that step,
that stockingless, sneakered step of mine,
was the angry word a fat man spoke
who suddenly appeared. Cheeks blotching, voice
shaky—'How can you, just step over a man like that
on your way to school?' (He must've seen my books.)
I completely took in his meaning. He was
wearing a thin-striped, cheap green suit; and he
was American, of course—it wasn't some Chinese or Dane
come to say 'They teach you this in your country,
to stack the humans, soaked flammable, at night
in the icy streets?' No: a fat man. But I
had no answer, and as he was gone when I glanced
behind me, I doubt that he did. He'd no right
to ask me that, either. Oh, he was *free*
to ask, if you like, as the wino was free to show
the universe how terribly he could hate
in shattering that single vase, himself. And perhaps
in some twin city to this one, some right
angle to the real, no foot could ever land
on the far side of so fouled a river. But in this one
it did, it found a pavement, I carried my life
unfractured past that smoking, falling life.
If it's unfractured to sit on a parkbench
still answering the fat man: 'Not I ever called the cops
on winos in the winter flopping
under my tenement stairs or in the hall-johns.
The Chinese laundryman next door, or the old piece-stitcher
who'd "just missed" union housing, maybe she did.'
And all the time knowing, if I lived there now,
my kids out on that stoop, I'd call, I'd have to call them.

So that was my answer, of many but not the last, and launched
at the apartment towers and awnings of Fifth Avenue.
Where was he living now, I wondered—not
the bum, of course. Oh, somewhere, here in the city . . .
As somebody said once, New York
is everything that is the case: the rich
up there, me here, these scavenging; you're free
to do—whatever you do do, in this city.
Those buildings, for example: I used to wonder
what jobs people had, who lived there, did anyone ask them?
No. The point is, nobody stopped them. Or if you're a wino
on all fours under the bench, who's going to come asking
'How can you do this?'—or rather, who'll answer you, stop you?
The grimed and shaky fingers rattle
more butts in their bag and scramble sideways, twine
sawing in flapping armholes. With vertigo,
I keep noticing what a tacit
sense of each other's picking-space they have,
like an old couple's gardening . . . The fat man,
the more I think, he must've worked
down there. And wouldn't he, carrying himself to work
or home fat and tired past the red-ringed
eyes, the weakly hugged pints of witch hazel, feel
how day and night all roads lie open, hate
them, hate the passersby too, at last
lash out at barelegged me? I think so. Of course
he took the easiest feeling to hand, to spit out.
It must have eased several rubbing-places, though! And I think
when he sees derelicts now, he may go back
to that morning, nodding his head with uneasy
satisfaction, remembering, still asking me *How can you?*

7

The Billboard Man

At sunup at the foot of Broadway
the Mohawk builders of cities pause
crossing the blue flaw. They see the whole
island carved by one glacier (a drop of vapor
still rising and falling far out on the back of the ocean).
They see the sunlight steam softly
on sheetmetal, thousands aloft in the rigging, tailor birds
stitching the sails and aqueducts of the city.

In midtown, billboards and marquees light and cloud
Broadway. Cleopatra unrolled once more
from her carpet, ape armies, interstellar wars
. . . the White Nile lets a feather fall.
Over the lobby, two billpaper profiles eye
each other, glazed and dumb as fish.
Below, in the dark, in the whir and bloom
of the orchestra, stamen stirs against pistil.

Noon. Twelve hours from this, the billboard man
will start uptown. Through the traffic island trees blurry children
wait for his ladders and ropes. White-visored, nocturnal,
he'll spin himself out like a wrecker's ball, his canvas
shirt zigzagged with caustics; he'll spit, dissolve,
peel back : a sky full of snowfields : then the first roll
DIRECT FROM BROADWAY, his star one-eyed or armless
as Venus . . . but where is the other Broadway she has seen?

For now, the sun feeds on detail. Its lens screws down
tighter; the coral-lipped face of the man
blowing smokerings grains minute by minute more
with pores, teeth, wrinkles; the fine print magnifies
in crumpled classifieds in trashcans. Or take
the afternoon shopping crowd itself,
its mind crammed with impure form, the litter
that raises its floating nest for further litter.

Tender, corroding, the last light honeycombs
its fine edge of cornice. Fruitcrates to curbside.
With a brasstriggered bar, the greengrocer rolls down
his gate. A silvery mist, that no one has ever explained
and every foreigner gapes at, begins to drift from the manholes.
. . . Faint sounds of dismantling. White domes
crumble, the paper masonry of bees. All night
the weaver's shuttle wings backward, the

blocks fall softly back. At the foot
of Broadway the billboard man begins his climb
up the traffic-staggered avenue. Past midnight
the mind's walls dissolve, he comes through
with his paste-pails and long-handled brushes
in his overalls stained with biology, Saturn's rings
passes through with his fire escapes dreaming of fires
come to paint Giotto's O in the place of the city.

The Street

A round eclipse, a pool-like dot of light
on my little sister's glasses, bangs, her dome-cheeked, solemn face
play-powdered in a tilting compact mirror.

The sun was just up on the east of Manhattan,
its first rays straight across the Broadway ridge,
our downhill street still drenched in deep blue shadow.

Between our bay window's copper-green mullions, we two
knew every crevice and lip of our stoopball, stickball street:
our own building, all-white; the well-to-do black families

in brownstones; and the one brownstone, catty-cornered across:
a "house." Geraniums by the teal blue door, stooprailings
sparkling with black paint, and the special Friday night detail

of rookie cops in their pearl grey uniforms. I knew
what it all meant, or some tender, *Cannery Row*
confection of it, from my father. No connection

with our nerve-splitting schoolyard world, where mean kids
shadow-terrorized, and the overhead grownup world
slowly lowered toward us all. A family joke, a "house . . ."

A cry of astonishment, "Look!" floated down
from Broadway. Then Vicky stood up, palms pressed
against the embrasure, and screamed. The sun

had just lifted, spilling and blazing downhill
off hubcaps, a hydrant's hexagonal arms, streaking shadows
pencil-tip-thin from the paving motes. On the sidewalk across

a girl from the house, in stockingfeet, dark silk suit
slit and ribboned by knife thrusts, was pulling herself
through the arcs and dribbles and splashes of her blood.

Her fingertips' carmine meshed on the concrete, her elbows strained
over the wet, working shoulderblades (one still hooked
through her pursestrap) and somehow her bluish felt

hat and hatpin, rolled to the curb, made me think she was pinned
to the street—pinned and moving. She was trying to hitch herself,
still with faint spurts of bleeding, up to the corner where

the Broadway passersby, clustering, slowing, stared down
at that maimed, insectile crawl. Beside me, Vicky was clenched tight
with willing someone to help. I was trying to marginally

shift her, to save her; if she were a girl from the brownstone
next door, say, just starting to work; or a Drive lady, out
for morning croissants— Below, the girl twisted her head

back toward the blue door (closed, blinds drawn)
and then took a shiver or sharp stitch of breath
that seemed to fling her limp in her silk slashes.

Vicky's head bumped the glass. My father, who'd stopped
loading his briefcase to look, pulled her sideways, but she
was saying, something Daddy go down (and I

never doubted, I saw him down there with a blanket), but he
what was he saying? To explain
why he didn't go down? For I certainly heard it, acted on it, grew

around it like treebark around one particular paling
below our street on the Drive (the grey freckled belt
of tree grown right over the haft and back).

Vicky tugged herself free. The compact went skittering down
to the carpet, its dot-quiver magnified
on a framed drawing, *Nude Boy with Horse*. The part of me

that records things for keeping has a blank then, as if
the city and its citizens—johns, rackets, pimps, the whole
purchased precinct lay silent around her

(only nearer, in familiar unfurnishedness booming, the parent voices
came on in the hallway, but muted, planetary—and somewhere
far out on the periphery, the sirens started). But we

had learned it all by heart by then—so swift to receive
her fading signals—perm, nails, the just-fit, once
of her suit. She'd worked to please the ones inside that house

and now the stiff pageboy lay tumbled—black threads of it
wetted red—her cheek on the place where shoes
walked, dogs stopped—this was what was, other things

what people said. And to that I must add, by our own stillness most of all
we were taught; from that we learned and learned.
As for the woman who'd spent herself pulse and veins

for a last inch of life, did she think it was all for her,
her sickness and bad fame, that no one came near? Her eyes
had opened on the unmoving watchers on Broadway. And last thing

before we were hauled from the window seat, we saw her
raise one terrible red-nailed arm
and wave to them, sign them to come down to her.

. . . Much later, and late for school, when we were sent down
onto the stoop, my sister's face still reddish
lost and bereft behind her rounds of glasses

the opposite walk was clear if we'd had to cross there,
only a dark calligraphy beneath a sheen of water,
one lingering cop to crank the hydrant closed.

The Key to the City

All middle age invisible to us, all age
passed close enough behind to seize our napehairs
and whisper in a voice all thatch and smoke
some village-elder warning, some rasped-out
Remember me . . . Mute and grey in her city
uniform (stitch-lettered JUVENILE), the matron
just pointed us to our lockers, and went out.
'What an old bag!' 'Got a butt on you, honey?' 'Listen,

did I get lost with these streetnames! Spruce
Street, Water, or get this, VANderwater—' Cautiously, coolly,
we lit up, crooking palms for the ashes. All fifteen
or under, all from Manhattan, we loitered bare
to the waist for the X-rays. In the whorling light
from one rainy window, our shapes were mere
outlines from floor to wall, opaque
as plaster, white, or terra-cotta, black . . .

'Names or numbers,' a skinny white girl with pale blue eyes
shrugged her shoulders. 'Why come here at all? You think little Susan
(thumb mockingly hooked at herself) needs working papers
to work in my uncle's diner? If they'd let me off school
at noon now—that's where the real tips are!'
And she smiled at our objections around her smoking
cigarette (I thought) like some museum mummy,
amber-fingered, fishhook collar bones—

'What are you talking? Don't you know the city
keeps like an eye we don't get overworked?'
'Yeah, and your Social Security number, that's
for life, girl, that ain't worth something to you?'
The skinny girl just cackled, goosepimpled arms
huddled against her ribs. 'Whadda you two, work
for the mayor? What's this (swinging her locker key
with its scarred wooden number)—the key to the city?'

She meant last week, when they'd offered it
to some visiting queen. Even I snickered. I
was younger than most of them, homesick among the near-
women's breasts and hair, even the familiar
girls' cloakroom odors: perspiration, powder, decades
of menstrual fust— 'Well, I'm coming back in six months.'
This was one of the black girls, elbow swivelled
on pelvic sidethrust, finest hair–

filaments, finerimmed, sulky mouth. 'She'll be
sixteen, getting married,' the girl next over
burst in eagerly, 'He got a store job, still her folks
against it, they say stay in school. But every
afternoon—' Distantly, the first girl listened to
her own story, only breaking in at the end: 'I want a real
church wedding. Down here is just for the license, see?'
'A license,' said "little Susan," sourly, 'like for a job?'

'His name is Harold Curtis,' was all she answered, then 'It too strong
for my parents. They see it too strong for them in the end.'
In our silence, the gutter slurred strangely. And for just one
moment, everyone breathless, the atmosphere grew
almost tender. But nobody knew what to say
except *good luck*, so we all went on smoking like chimneys
except the one murmur, of old and incurable
anger, 'Listen. Listen. They get you coming and going.'

Now each girl tilts her face down, contemplating
her own unseen choices, real
tips, the solitary and common
square foot of imaginary chance . . . Outside, the rain
was letting up. The city, like a graph
of its own mountainous causes, climbed in a mist
across our window. And then the matron came, calling
our locker numbers, one by one, for the X-rays.

'Jesus, it's late.' 'Hey honey, *I'm* ready!' 'Where'd we change
at from the D Train?' Through the clearing air on the far
side of City Hall Park, I could see a narrow street
and a streetsign: Broadway. Miles to the north
my street had a number, and Broadway was really broad.
In the concrete prows of islands, the innumerable old women
were sitting, lonely as soldiers, silent as . . .
'What's up, girl? Goose step on your grave?'

Another number. And now, the room darker, each girl
cast about for the cheering word, when 'Listen,' I suddenly
heard my own voice saying, 'Guess what I saw coming down? A street
called Anne Street.'—'So what?'—'So my name is Anne.'
A pause, then 'Hey kid, that's really funny!' They all
grinned, and one of the older girls gave my shoulder
a tolerant punch. I was one of the youngest, and as far
as I can remember, that was all that I said.

The Lenses of Jacob Riis

(*The turn-of-the century reformer and photographer, for whom the housing project on Avenue D is named*)

It stills like a retina now, these black
and silver photographs, cool residue
of an anger more searching than art. Slowed
by your lenses' gravity, the feeble glare
of flashlight-and-frypan, a ring of grimed faces
stares out from a Mott Street cellar
below tidewater, crammed with lodgers and coal.
Then more backtenements, more
warrens and roosts of the poor wards.
You photographed them
for annihilation only, and so we see them now,
here by the river:
feral faces through gratings, wan faces
flooding from laundries of shade . . .

                          The evidence,
as it dripped from pins in your darkened kitchen:
fresh lantern slides for the Board of Health.
Yet to you the ring showed itself ever
Tammany-formal, from the inaugural
bandstand to grinning and hatted
street Arabs palming a single butt.
Like a watermark: the Bohemian uncles
binding cigars, the seamstresses
in night lofts sewing through endless shifts.

But especially the immigrant families, their
eyes small and wild with the New World,
upright in their circle, limned like trees
in your lenses' angry, archaic light.

16

A Grade School History

It's only at night now I cross the Line
where once I crossed to school each morning:
our paradigm of difference, Broadway. One block
from the plane trees of Riverside Drive,
then one more raddled block to the school
and Amsterdam—really Harlem. Stooprails
with black spikes and tendrils; lead-green
entryways hurried by
in the drowned light of winter, each with its pale egg hung
from one weedy cord. One death there, a child's, was for me
enough to swell airwells and landings
with children's faces distorting for air; while two blocks west
the sun set through leaves and bay windows
on the thousand hand-tied crimsons of a carpet
where a visiting child, perhaps,
lay reading. Only one
of the lines of difference that drop across
the very birthlines and cut them; not with the first
breath that inflates the squashed lungs but later, sharper, across
the Line we hear the blues fill up
the summer night, the Public Enemy
exhaling his different air.

                                 Mornings, I went to my "Merit job"
in the Nurse's room. 'Who ironed your dress so pretty?'
she asked the first day. 'The maid.' I thought the highschool girl
who helped with my stepmother's wash twice a month
was what the Drive kids called the maid (*our* windows looked over
    Broadway).
'Your mother couldn't be bothered, hmn?' Then I saw
I was wrong, I didn't try to explain
where my mother was, the wrong was where I was,
on their side, the school's side, of the Line.

I was like *Haarlem,* in our fifthgrade United States
history—out of focus, and weird. At the end of the section
on Slavery, the city had 'more Negroes
than any African capitol. At the density
of Central Harlem, all America could fit
into the rest of Manhattan.' All America! I underlined that
with the first ball point I owned. And then it all turned
into a dream; I still have it; I'm going ice-skating
east of Broadway, and as I cross over the city
seems to enfold me: sun muted, somewhere the pitchless ring
of ashcan on curbstone, voices from gated sills . . . Then of course the
dreamfeeling changes. The street dissolves east
to its grimmest and densest quarters. Illustrated horrors
of the Middle Passage: the slaves crouched too close on their grid
to sit or lie down; tongues swollen, extruded; their eyes in the placid
        whorls of a period engraving staring
up from the page . . . Half-waking, I grasp
my forgotten color; I know some day Time will lift me
out, by the hand, from his terrible oubliette.

                                        'Anne. Whatever happens,
stay put,' the Nurse said one morning. The hall bells
kept ringing. I sat in her chair, to better enjoy the being
alone there, and somehow protected. I stared at her charts
of lymph, of nerves, the circulation
of the blood. Three stories above me a scream
had drawn girls into the boys' room
to stare at the shoes turning slowly, as the boy
turned on the cubicle's crossbar—the thinsoled,
thickpolished shoes. At the Nurse's steps
they scattered, taking word to every room
that he hung by a 'ratty old sashcord,' his own
Patrol belt, or 'a big man's tie,' that he was
black, a sixthgrader, the same kid who'd once set fire
to his homeroom wastebasket . . . Next day, we had to unearth

his permanent file. 'This child is troubled,'
one teacher said. 'No attention.' 'Troublemaker,' and so on.
Though lately he'd been quieter, 'a disturb
influence,' his mother, having died. And filling up with that
and too much other difference, at last
it became entirely him . . . That was all. His eyes
in the file photograph said
no thoroughfare to mine—sad
with looking out from the terribleness that is.
He had no story now. He'd turned into part
of mine, or the school's, or my sister's second grade class, afraid
to raise hands for the john . . . I ran faster
past the strongsmelling stoops. Or even decades
later, my mind going blank at a phrase
from the Haitian slavetrade in somebody's
memoirs: 'Les Ibo se pendent,' the Ibo hang themselves—unsuitable
for grade school histories. (It was
a tie that he used, though, a man's tie. I saw it
later on in the office.)

                    Now the Nurse's phone
rang endlessly: inquiries, forms; now the rest of Manhattan
wanted cause and solution, one page in the book of Harlem . . . The
     teachers
said smaller classes. A school psychologist. The Mayor
would speak the boy's eulogy. A strung-up black teacher slapped me
for slapping a roach off my black friend Rachel's
shoulder—'A likely story!' As for my dreams, I ought to
have lost, as a luxury, my freedom of the black
capitol within our capitol. But I went on
crossing there nightly, while in its own time the city
made its recommendation: a brand new "Merit slot"
for the Nurse's room. So I had company that year,
my last at the school. But the Mayor never
visited us that winter, I never saw him come driving

19

up the Line and turning east with the street
past the sweatered women in doorways, the stoop-bolted men.
He came there years later, though, my father read it out
from the *Times*. As news to exiles returned, already
half-illegible in this, the real life: he read it:
the Mayor visited our school, and no
connection, no eulogy, but it seems a rat
ran across the stage while he was talking and this
is what he said: There are no rats. Somebody
must have caught this one and let it loose on me
just to make trouble.

The Ruins

In shorts and sneakers, torso's weight caught
on the bent left leg, palm flat on the granite flutings
you crouch on a fragment of lintel. Loose masonry
flours your hams, your calves, the right knee elbow-hooked
against the sparrowy black ribcase. You bask economically,
    shoulderblades tilted
to catch the last sun. Singularities: the eyes slightly
protuberant, underlid reddish and wet; a slate-blue
vein in the eyebrow. Expression: furious, inward, fixed.

Across the street, boarded tenements; on this side
a level campus of rubble: brickmounds, a worn
topscrim of silver and cellophane. At Eighth Avenue, one building's
still upright, stapled shut with a lustrous
sheet of industrial grade aluminum. By the stoop, an afghaned
armchair, a telephone table; here innerness and the street
begin to converge . . . On the UNFIT FOR HABITATION sign
HUMAN is spray-painted over with DOG.

The New York Times, May 6—"Some streets might have ceased to be part
of the city. No police, fire protection; TB everywhere; heroin; in three
    blocks
studied by the Times, the chance for a normal death
for anyone is one in twenty." A man on a step is interviewed:
"The social workers left. The garbage trucks left. The Red Cross left."
Then a "lay worker" (this is poetry): "To our demented inn, the world,
the LORD came uninvited. And only in these
disinherited, does He hide Himself—for whom there was no room."

So Heaven and Earth have put their hands to the work
that holds this boy, and holds him on this block. Not one
light swerves of thousands outbound on the East Side Drive, or reflected
in the shady vitrines of Madison, of Park; ten minutes

on the A Train from air-conditioning, residential
towers still half I-beams, the endlessly pinwheeling brush-
points of A *Starry Night,* and can not one of these
banks of incandescence cast a lightline to these ruins?

Candle saucers start yellow smears in the chickenwired
windows of the corner tenement. It is dark now, and somewhere out in
     the dark
a landlord overtightens a pressure valve. Clean rounds of brick
where Con Ed stripped the meters; a greenish mineral
floodstain where addicts hacksaw copper pipes
and strip the burst boiler for salvage. Signs, straws
in the wind, like the hairline rust circles
next to the hydrants where women set down their pails.

The capital itself (they say) has fled the city
that once expressed itself in rows
of dumbbell tenements. Now insurance costs dictate
they must seem to fall from within. One chance
in twenty . . . No, no god has elected your life. Nothing's hidden inside
     you
but your dying childhood, and whatever is on its way
from the outside to replace it. Streetlight falls
like streaks of drypoint around the tight, huddled limbs.

Expression: obscure now, lid-glistening, as if
you'd tried to seal yourself into something
separate, and when this is denied a flatness
comes into the human face. Yet it's only the armor
of outside, still inlaid with its useless and lovely
uniqueness of inside. Almost you weep, taking arms, and one day
one source of your street cool will be this tear
spread without depth or relief over the whole eye.

The Armada

Elizabeth Near and Far

The Stethoscope

Like Halley's comet, bending on its tail,
you curl beneath the black cup on my skin:
I guess at limbs in half-eclipse, obscure
and fluent as a distant telegram.
Unworldly, small, sealed orders, darkroom heat,
soon among the signals pulsed, the static whoosh, arrives
in distant thuds your rapider than human
heartbeat—sex unknowable—bud eyes—

Yet of our world you only know the tree
you lie beneath, its root your belly, fronds
and villi falling in the sunken lake
of capillaries, bubbles, breathing bonds . . .
I sigh. And somewhere you incline your vast
night-sighted brow—your jointed, swimming hands—

Night Light

Only your plastic night light dusts its pink
on the backs and undersides of things; your mother,
head resting on the nightside of one arm,
floats a hand above your cradle
to feel the humid tendril of your breathing.
Outside, the night rocks, murmurs . . . Crouched
in this eggshell light, I feel my heart
slowing, opened to your tiny flame

as if your blue irises mirrored me
as if your smile breathed and warmed
and curled in your face which is only asleep.
There is space between me, I know,
and you. I hang above you like a planet—
you're a planet, too. One planet loves the other.

25

The Chair by the Window

Your rhythmic nursing slows. I feel
your smile before I see it: nipple pinched
in corner of mouth, your brimming, short, tuck-cornered
smile. I shake my head, my *no* vibrates
to you through ribs and arms. Your tapered ears
quiver, work faintly and still pinker, my
nipple spins right out and we
are two who sit and smile into each other's eyes.

Again, you frowning farmer, me your cow:
you flap one steadying palm against my breast,
thump down the other, chuckle, snort, and then
you're suddenly under, mouth moving steadily, eyes
drifting past mine abstracted, your familiar
blue remote and window-paned with light.

Elizabeth Near and Far

You are awake, held in arms, chin
balanced on my shoulder, small globe turning back
while mine much larger faces straight ahead.
It sounds as if you'd found your thumb—you thrum
inward, but audible: *frrum, frrum,* you're talking.
I sense your eyes go past me and around
your thumb to where some floating speck of light
hovers, microscopic, in your glistening gaze.

Or mornings when you lie awake, your first
faint vowels floating up (the nursery door ajar).
You place your hands on air; push, croon, turn,
all softly, all alone (my head half-in the door)
and stroke the wall and murmur in the still-
shaded room, and are alone with yourself.

Pregnant Woman Reading Letter

These Navigations and hours of sailing
are indistinct with distance.
Cloudy with India ink your
landfall itself evaporates, the irrigation
canals flow placidly south, one sail
carried back through the calendar
of harvests and doors, cities of inundation.
Yet the edges of your thought
are crisp with age and hard to touch,
as if you were not growing younger.

And my head as I read this seems to project
into the lower quadrant of a wall-map
unrolling from somewhere out of sight above me.
Sagging with gravity, the inked networks
of rivers hang downward, the coastlines, the
unintelligible continents . . . It is as if
an unearthly shadow fell from me:
the planet unfolding out of the map
like a blown cloak full of faces
my right hand lying huge on the sun
the other dark in the moon's clarities.

Paolo Uccello

The Battle of San Romano

Under the black leaves of the orange grove,
a moonlit cannery of mail and visors
and condottiere with rapt, inward smiles.
Their horses rear, snowy among the flowers,
their forelegs seem to graze a world without motion;
only the Florentines' scarlet banner
and the lemony spears of the spearmen
move in the dark vanishing point of the trees.

So each heart found its own desire
at the *Battle of San Romano*,
but especially the brachet and the hare,
they thought they were a tapestry,
and the helmet that floated off and grew small,
discovering perspective.

The Deluge

Here everything is leisurely but the perspective
hurtles backward at the speed of light
whirling off damp drapery and color
from the numberless blank-bodied
nudes. But not to imitate,
but initiate, the breathing world,
does every plank and painted bear converge:
none enter here without geometry.

His mind on the vanishing point,
Uccello squats like Descartes in his oven.
But God hangs down headfirst
into the painting, astonished at His world
that has simply picked up and gone
in receding lines, following the Piper.

The Lost Frescoes of San Miniato

Now everyone in Vasari works all night
with a candle in his cap and his feet in shavings
and is "reclusive" or "sophistical."
But who else has a houseful of paper
birds, of *uccelli*, whose Muse is a wooden sphere
with seventy-two hand-shaved facets?
Even on San Miniato's
Byzantine walls, you graphed out

a third dimension, diminishing
your frescoed towns to perfection,—then colored them pink.
"Which is a great fault," says the oracle,
"for stone is grey, but all he had to eat was cheese."
. . . And still your sleepy wife calls you to bed,
and still *Ah wife* you cry *What a sweet thing is this perspective.*

Alternate Lives

Tired of trying to become
a morning of study   a snowy morning of study
as if snow papered lips and hair
and lightened the myriad numbers and genders
(*but there is a fish as dark as me a bird*)
and all my papery profiles glowed and lightened

but the alternate lives call each on one clear tone
and the mind drifts backward like a paper boat
fragrant as this morning's treetrunks—
"Night Watchman Wanted"   "Furnished Room to Rent"
then sailing on through the wall it leaves you
in the interior miles from human   you gave

new laws to the trees in tears these are my people
rough face streaming knotholes centennial rings
last glimpsed towards twilight by a rare
traveller to that brown north land—where an oar
is a winnowing fan the moon a handful of feathers—
a tiny trousered shape across the fathoms of distance

and still the alternate lives descend
depthless and even-handed   still the line
of lighteyed bearded old women reappears
these lives honed down to three or four obsessions
these armchairs and grey arms that stream
slow television light . . .

even language grew too young to follow
nights alone in the tiny rented room
with the Polestar at the window   too huge   too white
dreaming still emptier rooms to dream
of rooms in—but at the far end
you saw the life those ancient lives projected

all your old neighborhoods are pasted over
with signs and arrows pointing to this hour
still you are not quite these not quite one breath
with the pleasant room the littered workdesk
that is for the snowstorm looking in
it knows what the good life is   so once did you.

Suburban Hours

Early morning in Cameron Lane
the husbands appear in the doorways,
upright and hatted silhouettes they cross
the limegreen lawns, the inkblue pools
of shadetrees, of ornamental shrubs—all Sunday
how the power mowers hummed and hovered—
slowly the husbands pass over the verge into daylight.
But inside the houses for women
pouring more coffee the lucid light
glistens on butter knives, reflects
the creamjug on its glazed blue tile.
We will move in this light a solid among solids.

Already the motions of dusting flow
alongside us like sculpture, the white stride
of hooded mannequins in *Vogue*;
whole mornings gleam down the linoleum squares
like colored fields to distant, cloud-hung kitchens.
Outside the house the hours pass
impalpably as light, silence . . . Our neighbor
glides from her house, mop extended, and the tree
she beats, the wooden mop, the hidden
trees in the walls of houses dimly thrum.

The light grows vertical, intense, trees blur. Somewhere
noon whistles signal from distant worlds.
The housewives are all in their houses.
One by one they abide in their dwellings
a mighty silence and a great quiet among them.
But the light speeds on across lawns
through conifers and windows. Brilliant
galaxies of dust appear, revolve
and vanish towards the shut lampblack
piano where the duster seemed to end.

Now the furniture opens its resonant mist, and this
is matter itself, dark systems, the nearest neighbor
a universe away. This is the house
spoken of, the house without walls or windows.

If we have remained immobile, it is the sun
that wheels its shafts through westward, level windows—
At my feet the tumbled capitals
on alphabet blocks and books resume their
shapes, their firm serifs: O with its clear elliptic
L, aloof, and A; musical thoughts
buried in daily speech. Then the tail
of C sweeps outward, the L lashes upright, the letters
swerve through the ropecolored air as if rosy eyes
as if lions or lionlike faces emerged
from the livingroom forest of sunlight.
It is the shapes of lions half-sunken in the walls.
It is only one lion but from every direction,
lions with faces lowering and golden
beards rumbling with aphoristic speech . . .

If you can walk out with this at moonrise
you will see the houselots along the Lane
rising and falling, darkly quilted and steepled.
As the round light climbs higher
your neighbors are toiling all around you
mouths closed and eyes open under the sky.
All night their laborious sleep
weaves tapestries undone all day behind

the signs of Chaud Soleil, Belle Vista and Wit's End.
At midnight their camelcolored lawns
crest up into dune-lit circles, crescents, loops:
here a cowled shape conversing with a centaur,
there a silvery beard in a darkened window.

33

At this hour the sun
lies deep below us, a buried plate, the moon
hangs far above, and we see the Lane
unwinding between them towards transparency.

The Illustrated Gazetteer

across the walled continent
at the back of the rainy horn-white mountains
reading the names of the rainsmoking towns over and over

at last my name dampens and slips away
from the motionless figure on the sofa
tonnage of thumb and forefinger slanting down

each morning this body for raising bodies
thoughts of leaden coffee   iron pans
how I am heavy heavy to get up

always dreaming more lonely and minimal lives
as Mercator shrinks the known world and the North
snows over mammoth continents

"the irrational punishments of matter" . . .
such I imagine the old age of the world
cracked walls   the plumbline and its shadow

for me it's this damned mule of a life   bloodshot eye
aiming body in jerks—lift the roof of any house
and you'll find six people brooding on the age

these names from the Gazetteer
came floating back like loose canoes
the cities closed their eyes

now each man seeks himself a hermitage
faraway deserts mountains and shores   and you
you too have come to long for these things

Day and Night in Virginia and Boston

After three months, Virginia is still a frontier.
Late at night, I close the door
on my husband practicing Mozart, the dishpan fills
and the network affiliates sign off one by one.
Now the country stations, tuning up like crickets
on radios in scattered valley kitchens:
Har yall this evenin folks!
(Wanting to say 'I'm real fine' I whisper 'Wow.')
Got your Green Hill chicory perkin'? An army
of women, straightened and ironed and blued
like Picasso's ironer—jerking coffeecups
back with one gesture, hips pressed to sinks.
Their suspendered husbands are reading—the paper? the Bible?
And it's *Jesus for you and for me*, till midnight—the anthem—
and one soaped hand jerks out, and their lighted lives recede
to kitchens on the moon's dark side, Mozart rising . . .
Daytimes, in post office, gas station, greasy spoon,
I don't see them anywhere, it makes me nervous.
Black faces down here look "colored."
I am afraid of the other, red faces.

Take my first job in Boston,
the outgoing typist said, 'You've got
to know the foms, we use so many foms.'
And I said *O why farms?*
I thought law firms had *torts.*
A tort, I thought, was like *vous avez tort.*
But I was wrong about the farms,
and after the Cardinal's Vietnam speech
one of the girls said, 'Think you're smat with that accent?'

Still, nothing soothes me, sometimes,
like American voices, softened with distance,
with nearness, as murmurs in a darkened Greyhound:
'It sure has been a scorcher.' 'Where you folks from?'

I keep yawning, lightworlds off in the dark . . .
Sometimes my lonesome standard English sleeps:
The varied and ample land, the North and South in the light,
and the voices of Earth and Moon swell in my helmet
with prairie inflections, soft twangs of outer speech—
'You're looking real good,' says Earth.
'—ain't that somethin'?'
'Roger. No sweat. Out.'

Readings in the Navigators

Jet Flight Frankfurt—New York

Haze and blue cubist fields
a thin sleeve of water, then twenty
minutes of England, then two
hours of the Atlantic.

Now, barely moving below us
at watches-back time, the Labrador barrens
snowy, seamed with glacial debris
have not ended yet.

Half the world is waste.
"The land God gave to Cain"
wrote Cartier. *The city below our left wing*
is a frostheave; what looks like a highway—

A shadow flies over the Ice Age.
The compass needle strains tensely, the pale face
in your window now profiles a carp
now a brow-plucked Florentine nun . . .

And handkerchiefs, tiny farms
float down through the dark:
'But that one's a highway.'
No. The movie has ended.

'Where are we?' 'Still over Labrador.'
'My God, look down, look at *that*.'
True homeland   world without fire
'When do we get to the city?'

Manhattan Schist

Palisades full of young fire
but not our weathered Manhattan
schist almost older than fossils
walls eyeletted and fishhooked
by the meltwater only.

As when a whole third of the world
still lay undiscovered: below in the ragged light
of the subway you'll find the same
blankness . . . There are circuits strung off
into nowhere down there, lost conduits, mains

that no one living has counted.
Like the conifer forest that grew here
long ago, on the back of the ice sheet.
It was full of birds and brown rivers—a kind
of history without history, perhaps.

Inwood Marble

North of the Cloisters, north of Dyckman,
the Inwood marble runs in where the schist
on the west drops away; the streets' ends are planked off
and stairways zigzag down from the backs of courts

to a lower, shabbier streetlevel ten stories down.
Here the city trails off into wreckers' yards, tin-roofed
garages overgrown with goldenrod and mallow
and knuckles of the paler seafloor stone.

Rustred of sidings, rustgreen of half-buried ties . . .
This is Hudson's island, carwash and tropical hush,
at the land's edge the cloudlike overhanging trees,
the cattails, and the brown-disked coneflower.

Nocturne

You resume your original
blackout, caves, the moon huge
on top of Brooklyn gazing into our face.
The green aisle of Third Avenue
echoes to human cries, and your skyline

"an Iland of plaintive musicke"
to the mariner's ear. But is this
the New World then? this floodlit
canvas sailing the Hudson? Then please
take us with you, wherever you're going—

wherever you're going. At midnight
the moon comes nearer the city
the skyscrapers fill with the rustling of brooms.
On the landings stone watchmen stare
here, in the horn of the wheat.

Demolition Crane

The brown cranes are here again, unpapering
room after room at the first hint of spring.
They have a new city in wraps, built itself
on flutes tall and slender as cranes.
But right now it's pure peace, one quarter
trails after another into vacant
gazes, grassy departures . . .

A large wicker birdcage is turning in the wind
on a corner off Sixth Ave. The light
changes, the blurred and exhausting roar
of the wind, the West Side, real crows
come to nest in your crowsnests.
And everything you say may be true, all our old

neighborhoods have grazed the horizon
where the Red Sea is wearing away
with its chalked names and doorbells, its twilights remoter
than China. But wherever a brick falls away
we can see the tiny clay cities clinging
perfect handfuls of dwelling, timeless, abandoned
from summer to summer like straws.

To New York

Always to arrive in this city
smoking estuaries   boatloads of dead tongues
     Manhattan backlands darkened with fluttering cloth
with your firescapes   mute childhoods   street-vendors
     behind all the faceless
and falling masonry of this quarter
     again and again your deep voice
breaks into its crabbed white script

     It might be on Twelfth Street
in the tiny Polish storefronts
     a circle of gold rims in the stovelight
and the immigrant airleaves unfolding into winter
     Nowy Swiat   Atlantis   Yiddishe Qual
—You nod, and all night it snows the numbers of streets
     with the voices heard high in the courtyard
and the creaking wind on the landings
     where women rise snowy-faced, owl-feathered . . .

Invisible city   hidden skyline flowing away
     like the shadow of walledup canals (yet with
what tenderness, what sadness, Ninth Avenue—
     dark moraine—   Tenth Avenue)
You are with the fled sounds
of sidewalks latches and waterways
     in our murmurs   in a tide of footfalls
in the Thieves' Alley enormous eyes pressed to windows—

Yet I came here for this, only for this
     driving endlessly North
into zone after zone of your densities, past
     the dwindling poles, attenuated threads
of thought growing purer and blanker
     treeline   nightline   perpetual, near . . .

(Detail)

A dusky cloud, a tree, a giant (caught on the line
of magnification) deeply whorled hand
from the painting's center. A picturesque little house
with watersteps and a boat, momentarily forsaken.
You can see its boatman down by the lagoon
with two others, pointing deeper into the painting

with a shrewd air of debate. *They've* never heard of painting;
that's why they convince us, themselves little more than a brushline
or two, a lick and a promise, that their bottle-green lagoon
can be sailed, the fish in it caught, the pointing hand
shaken. The boat's only temporarily forsaken.
But since the detail's so sharp, shall we look at the house

itself? The easy, sleazy, grassgrownover house?
Of course it's a bit rundown, could do with repainting.
It must be the window that makes it look so forsaken,
a lick of cloth inside one square dark line
that opens nothing, opens onto nothing . . . Hand
labor is certainly not what it was. Look at the lagoon:

seen closer, a lovely color, but as a lagoon?
And could this chimney-narrow cottage really house
even tenants much smaller than that monstrous hand?
So rustic, so swallowed up in the landscape, painting
might hardly exist. (It hardly does.) There ought to be a line,
somehow, between a place that's just forsaken

looking, and something much worse than forsaken:
not meant to be lived in at all, no more than that lagoon.
Not even meant to deceive, past a certain point.
Look at those boatmen, yarning below the house
—we thought, but they're done without mouths in the painting.
This is not sight (we must hope) but oversight, the master's hand

too immersed in its mythological theme (some offhand
Shipwreck of Ulysses, no doubt, or *Ariadne Forsaken*)
to dwell on the rest. Our very seeing this part of the painting
is an accident, but none who've looked on this lagoon
look back. They have seen the intention thin, thin house
flat boat and empty canvas sail across the Line.

You'll even forget what you wanted: the hand to cup the lagoon
its people and boats unforsaken, a solid house,
a painting you could believe in its every last line.

Prayer for Peace

Heavy, —ineffectual, —these are old words:

Kyrie, eleison.

Lord, mercy.
Lord, peace.
What is so stale with being known yet so effectively
unknown as this: Lord, not without, but within:
the dreadful, yearning
Collective behind the eyes,
interlocking, there, with all the other yearnings—

(Impalements at doorposts; Lent vigils; Plague in the prairie town traced
to gopher holes on the searchlight-swept installation.)

        *   *   *

My Lord and my only God,

give peace. If it were not so infinitely
dangerous. Mercy. Parts of the mind like the
cell-tainted rock of the primitive *secretum*
or crypt—from which, and of like substance, the evenly
incrementing ribs; others the clerestory hung
in its planetary, possible half of light.

My Lord, whom are we addressing? Like language, made through a
history, like breath through the body? A communal
creation, representing worlds
of invested labor . . . How can we pray, then, burning
as we do to adore yet adoring
whatever burns?—each emotion, each prayer, reversing

to its beautiful, ominous dorsal fin· solitary arch
above waters: in the made desolation this inward, backward wave.

45

The Hall of Armor

On first reflection, all these polished knights
go back to the caveman's obsession: how to be in and out
of the cave at once. It's sad to see the armor
trying to imitate knees with a splay of lames
or elbows with an oiled bronze wheel. It knows all
outlets, eyes, say, are inlets, and like the river that armed
Achilles, it hardly knows where to stop. As for the foe
of course it's the body itself, which rules out
the ideal suit of armor, a burnished, seamless
lozenge of Toledo steel.

                   From closer in
you can see that the armor is trying to make it up
somehow, to the body. There are garlands engraved
on the mirrored plates, Latin mottoes and fleurs-de-lys.
One suit even has a complete
Repos du Guerrier, a knight
asleep among nodding grasses.
Step closer. The armor stands arms
open, incised with shimmering sprays, reflecting a world
of meadows and afternoons. And almost
you might drift off in these arms, but above
the huge beetle face peers down, melancholy
as if a voice from within whispered *I am lonely*.

The Armada

Through the meridian's fine blue hairlines, the admirals are converging
in their fish-hulled ships, with their frogmen and sirens, and tanks with
      knotted chain flails
that beat the ground before them as they crawl.

Behind them the cities dim out, on the foredeck the admirals sigh
to lean from the curving bows, to trail
their fingertips in the water . . .

All alone on the landmass, the Ship's Artist simply draws what he sees:
red men with arms like flesh clubs, blue-daubed men with parasol feet
and fish with weeping human faces. The sonic boom arrives at his feet

in the palest ripples. In the painting, Gloriana rides under arms
towards Tilbury Town. Her profile shimmers in the sodium lights
that seem to cast no shadows before or behind her.

Like compass pencils of light, their fingertips spread out
the nervous systems more complex than spiral nebulae.
Orchards of mines grow up on the ocean floor.

Now under radar they study the green road glowing
and add a late-rising moon. The sea so full of maprooms, and the cliffs
chalked with weaponry symbols, trailing the phosphorescence of
      minesquads.

Only the grassblown Norman ringmounds go on dreaming
of Monet picture hats and streaming scarves,
the bunker disguised as a picnic, that went on forever.

Now the Cathedral at Bayeux, with its windows and views, is rolled up
and the Conqueror's navy on its blue worsted waves
and Hengist and Horsa, the Escorial with its green shoals of ships, all are
      safely rolled up.

Behind the Atlantic Wall, that Rommel called "Cloud–Cuckoo–Land,"
      the white-and-liver cows
moo through the milky light. The human faces carved
on Norman beams face out to the sea, which has grown

this answering forest of rigging. And very soon, just as soon
as the sea can see the land and the land the sea
the two of them will go to war.